ZAMBIA
STRUGGLES OF MY PEOPLE,
2nd EDITION

I0102981

VOLUME ONE

MULTIPLE CHOICE TEST BANK

Charles Mwewa

ACP PRESS

Africa in Canada Press
Toronto
2017

ZAMBIA

Struggles of My People, 2ⁿᵈ Edition
Volume One

MULTIPLE CHOICE TEST BANK

AFRICA IN CANADA PRESS

www.africaincanadapress.com

Author: Charles Mwewa, www.charlesmwewa.com
Typesetting and design by: Charles Mwewa
Cover design by: PowerBrain, South Africa
Printing: Africa in Canada Press

ISBN: 978-1-988251-18-9 (Canada)

ISBN-10: 1988251184

CONTENTS

ABOUT ZAMBIANIZATION 101

This course may be referenced as **Zambianization 101**. It is based on the five major themes and six competences contained in the three volumes of *Zambia: Struggles of My People*. It is designed to be a 52 weeks' course taken either online, or, where participating institutions are available, in-class situations.

Five Themes:

The themes illustrate:

#1: That democracy and development in Zambia cannot be adequately defined without taking into consideration Zambia's uniqueness and historical factors that impact upon its culture, society and future well-being;

#2: That a definite change of mind-set is essential if Zambia is to manipulate its people, natural and financial resources into productivity;

#3: That generational disparity exists in Zambian leadership formation that affects the choice of developmental models and for the most part, limits its investment, innovativeness and technological proficiency;

#4: That a combination of, or hybrid, ideological and pragmatic approach is necessary to unlocking Zambia's economic potential; and

#5: That a belligerent approach espoused by the International Financial Institutions, Cooperating Partners and the donor governments pre-empts Zambia's most coveted inventiveness, sophistication and free experimentation.

Six Competences:

In addition to the five themes, the course is instituted on the following six competences:

#1: To demonstrate an understanding of the history of Zambia;

#2: To demonstrate an understanding that the growth and stability of the Zambian economy depends on the critical scrutiny of past and present developmental models and the appreciation of the national-specific nuances that have a direct impact upon the strategies and mechanism that must aim at the eradication of poverty and social disillusionment;

#3: To demonstrate an understanding and appreciation of the necessity of respect for, and audacious pursuance of, democratic tenets and their impact on political development;

#4: To demonstrate the necessity for adherence to, and the appreciation for, liberty in the framework of human rights, freedom and inter-tribal amity as basis for national development, social integration and political and cultural hegemony;

#5: To understand and appreciate that the inculcation of sound moral and ethical good through education, religion and conscience are key to the unlocking of potential, leading to enlightenment, spiritual ascendancy and human actualization;

And #6: To demonstrate the understanding that law and the rule of law are cardinal in the ordering and stabilizing of society and the general good.

How to use this Test Bank

Instructors and Professors

This Test Bank offers a ready resource for adaption to any mode of class instruction. Instructors may provide guidance to students on how to define the Key Words/Phrases as well as how to tackle the Review Questions. If used specifically for assessment reasons, Instructors may not expose this Test Bank to students until theTests are completed and handed in.

Students

This Test Bank may be used by students who wish to assess their own understanding of the materials contained in Volum 1 of the 2nd Edition, *Zambia: Struggles of My People*. Where appropriate, students should hide the suggested responses and compare with their own separate responses. If available, participating students may submit the Review Question responses to participating institutions for grading.

Chapter 1 | Zambian Independence

Theme: #1
Competence: #1

Key Words

1. Independence
2. Self-determination
3. Struggle

Review Question/s

1. "Struggle is a journey and not a destination." Discuss.

2. Explain the meaning of "The attainment of independence was merely stage one in our common journey called Zambia!"

Multiple Choice

#1	Who was Zambia's first president?	Answer
A	Mainza Chona	
B	Harry Nkumbula	D
C	Arthur Wina	
D	Kenneth Kaunda	

#2	All of these are founding fathers of the Republic of Zambia. Which of them is NOT a founding father?	Answer
A	Edgar Lungu	
B	Kenneth Kaunda	A
C	Reuben Kamanga	
D	Harry Nkumbula	

#3	The first founding fathers of the Republic of Zambia were christened _____	Answer
A	Zambian A Team	
B	The Young Turks	A
C	Freedom Fighters	
D	Pioneers	

#4	Who was Zambia's first vice-president?	Answer
A	Reuben Kamanga	
B	Simon Kapwepwe	A
C	Mainza Chona	
D	Godfrey Miyanda	

#5	U.N.I.P stand for	Answer
A	United Nations Independence Party	
B	United National Independent Party	C
C	United National Independence Party	
D	United National Indigenous Party	

#6	Who was the Minister of Power, Transport and Works during the construction of the TAZARA?	Answer
A	Aaron Milner	
B	Ben Mwila	A
C	Enoch Kavindele	
D	Simon Kapwepwe	

#7	Which of these countries both became independent in 1964?	Answer
A	Botswana and Lesotho	
B	Malawi and Zambia	B
C	Algeria and Burundi	
D	Rwanda and Egypt	

#8	The most recent country to become independent in Africa is _____	Answer
A	Angola	
B	South Africa	C
C	South Sudan	
D	Sudan	

#9	Kwacha means _____	Answer
A	Night	
B	Dawn	B
C	Shadows	
D	Morning	

#10	Ngwee means _____	Answer
A	Light	
B	Night	A
C	Shadows	
D	Here	

#11	On October 23rd, 1964, Kenneth Kaunda was _____	Answer
A	Prime Minister of Northern Rhodesia	
B	President of Northern Rhodesia	A
C	Prime Minister of Zambia	
D	President of Zambia	

#12	The Union Jack is _____	Answer
A	Zambian colonial flag	
B	Northern Rhodesia flag	C
C	British flag	
D	Symbol of oppression	

#13	The Zambian National Anthem sings to the tune of *Nkosi Sikelele Africa* (God Bless Africa). This tune was composed by _____	Answer
A	Enoch Sontonga	
B	The Black Mambazo	A
C	Kapasa Makasa	
D	Mama Kankasa	

#14	Each of the following applies to Evelyn Dennison Hone, except _____	Answer
A	Last Governor of Northern Rhodesia	
B	Keen sympathizer of Kaunda	D
C	Invited Kaunda to form the first Black government	
D	No college is named after him in Zambia	

8

#15	According to Grotpeter, the flag of Zambia means all these, except ____	Answer
A	It was introduced to Zambians in June 1964 by Kenneth Kaunda	
B	Its base color is green, representing the grassland of the country and its agricultural products, and the orange stripe symbolizes the country's (copper) mineral resources, and black represents the color of most of the population, and the red stripe is symbolic of the blood shed for freedom	D
C	The eagle in flight represents Zambian freedom	
D	Burning the flag is a criminal offence punishable by death	

#16	Who said these words: "Change does not roll in on the wheels of inevitability, but comes through continuous struggle. And so, we must straighten our backs and work for our freedom"?	Answer
A	Abraham Lincoln	
B	Martin Luther King, Jr.	B
C	Barack Obama	
D	Martin Luther	

#17	Zambian leaders chose October 24th as the date of Zambia's independence at ____	Answer
A	Lancaster House	
B	Mulungushi Rock of Authority	A
C	Mulungushi Conference Center	
D	Manda Hill	

#18	On which date was the United Nations (UN) created?	Answer
A	April 28th, 1945	
B	October 24th, 1945	B
C	October 23rd, 1945	
D	November 11th, 1945	

#19	Who gave to Kenneth Kaunda a kente cloth toga which he was dressed in at independence?	Answer
A	Kwame Nkrumah	
B	Julius Nyerere	A
C	Milton Obote	
D	Nelson Mandela	

#20	*Basungu* (singular: *Musungu*), which is a transliteration of the Swahili, *Wazungu*, literally means _____	Answer
A	People who move around	
B	People of color	A
C	Europeans	
D	South Africans	

Chapter 2 | My Zambia

Theme: #2
Competence: #5

Key Words/Phrases

1. Class Leadership
2. Kabundi
3. Kapisha Hotspring
4. Luano
5. Multipartism
6. Wamuyayaya

Review Question/s

1. Explain why education is a great equalizer; specifically, how it leverages wealth and reduces the gap between the haves and have-nots.

2. Discuss why a healthy nation needs well-equipped book libraries in various and accessible places.

Multiple Choice

#1	In the 1990s, the two most prestigious secondary schools in Zambia to where students who had obtained highest grades were sent were ____	Answer
A	Matero Boys and Kenneth Kaunda	
B	Hillcrest and Munali	D
C	Ibenga Girls and St. Raphael's	
D	Hillcrest and David Kaunda	

#2	When did Zambia return to multiparty democracy?	Answer
A	1990s	
B	2000s	A
C	1970s	
D	1980s	

#3	"All people are born equal, except that both ____ and ____ seem to set one person or a group of people apart from the other."	Answer
A	Information; culture	
B	Education; talent	D
C	Information; race	
D	Education; information	

#4	*Buyantanshi* may mean all these, except ____	Answer
A	Progress	
B	Movement	D
C	Forward	
D	Going backwards	

5	The atmosphere preceding the 1991 MMD electoral victory was such that Zambians would be all these, except _____	Answer
A	Wellbeing	
B	Sound in health	C
C	Savvy in technology	
D	Improved in living standards	

#6	Which shanty-town was once considered the cleanest in Zambia?	Answer
A	Kapisha	
B	Kapoto	A
C	Soweto	
D	Missisi	

#7	Where do you find Luano Primary School in Zambia?	Answer
A	Kitwe	
B	Chongola	B
C	Ndola	
D	Lusaka	

#8	Who was Edward Shamutete?	Answer
A	Former CEO and Chairman of ZCCM	
B	Founder of ZCCM	A
C	Former Chairman of Mpelembe Properties Limited	
D	Mayor of Chingola	

#9	In the 1980s, President Kaunda, gave a _____ subsidy for mealie meal to the Zambian poor.	Answer
A	Seed	
B	Warranty	D
C	Food	
D	Coupon	

#10	Zambia's staple cone/maize meal is known as _____	Answer
A	Millet	
B	Nshima	B
C	Soghum	
D	Mashola	

#11	Clothing wrappers worn by most women in Zambia are called _____	Answer
A	Kente	
B	Toga	C
C	Chitenge	
D	Buubu	

#12	President Kaunda of Zambia was famously known for waving his _____ handkerchief:	Answer
A	Black	
B	Green	C
C	White	
D	Orange	

#13	The Bemba proverb of "Umwana ashenda atasha nyina ukunaya" is emblematic of _____ :	Answer
A	Pride	
B	Mobility	B
C	Parenthood	
D	Legality	

#14	Each of the following were luxuries in Kapisha Compound, except	Answer
A	Radio	
B	Television	D
C	Meat	
D	Mangoes	

#15	Lack of information leads to lack of innovation and independent rational thinking. In societies where access to information is limited or non-existent, _____ and _____ rank high.	Answer
A	Poverty; misinformation	
B	Desperation; ignorance	C
C	Poverty; ignorance	
D	Violence; mistrust	

#16	In which year was the boys-only Hillcrest Secondary Technical School changed to Hillcrest High School co-education?	Answer
A	1992	
B	1994	B
C	1990	
D	2000	

Chapter 3| Political Activism

Theme: #1,2,3 & 4
Competences: #2, 4 & 5

Key Words/Phrases

1. Activism
2. Community Organization
3. Operation Young Vote (OYV)
4. Student
5. UNZA Closures
6. UNZA-IFEC
7. ZAMCAN

Review Question/s

1. "Students contributed to the end of colonialism."
   Discuss.

Multiple Choice

#1	In what year did UNZA open its doors to the first students?	Answer
A	1965	
B	1966	B
C	1964	
D	1973	

#2	What does O.Y.V stand for?	Answer
A	Operation Youth Voice	
B	Operation Young Vote	B
C	Open Young Vote	
D	Order and Youth Victory	

#3	How many UNZA closures occurred between the 1st and 2nd Republics?	Answer
A	4	
B	7	C
C	5	
D	6	

#4	The 3rd UNZA closure was instigated by student dissatisfaction and protestation against the _____	Answer
A	Ministry of Education	
B	UNZA administration	D
C	UNZASU executive	
D	Institute of Human Relations/Humanism	

#5	An organization that coordinates the social and cultural affairs of Zambians in Canada is called _____	Answer
A	ZAMCAN	
B	CANZAM	A
C	Zambian Canadian Organization	
D	Zambian Canadian High Commission	

#6	According to President Frederick Chiluba, what were students dissatisfied with and which led to most UNZA closures?	Answer
A	Meal allowances	
B	Government	B
C	UNZA administration	
D	Quality education	

#7	Who was UNZA's first Vice-chancellor?	Answer
A	Lungwangwa	
B	Serpel	C
C	Anglin	
D	Bussieres	

#8	Which world leader had benefited immensely from community organizing?	Answer
A	Hillary Clinton	
B	Robert Mugabe	C
C	Barack Obama	
D	Donald Trump	

#9	Since when have students been a political force in Zambia's democratic and political self-determination quest?	Answer
A	1960s	
B	1980s	A
C	1990s	
D	2000s	

#10	One of the biggest challenges identified in this book which Zambian community organizers face in the Diaspora is the idea of _____	Answer
A	"Zambian Time"	
B	Unity	A
C	Donations	
D	Attendance at meetings	

#11	The University of Zambia (UNZA) lifestyle may teach all these, except _____	Answer
A	Balance	
B	Order	B
C	Independence	
D	Cooperation	

#12	All these categories of people exist at UNZA, except ____	Answer
A	BAs	
B	Monks	D
C	Mojos	
D	Monk Sausage	

#13	All of the following persons have been UNZASU presidents, except ____	Answer
A	Kelvin Hambwenzya	
B	Simambo Banda	D
C	Jones Mwewa	
D	Fred Mmembe	

#14	Students have _____	Answer
A	Moral but not political rights to agitate	
B	Political but not moral rights to agitate	C
C	Both moral and political rights to agitate	
D	Only political right to agitate	

#15	Zambia and Canada's bilateral relations date back to _____	Answer
A	1964	
B	1966	B
C	1976	
D	2015	

Chapter 4| Rural Poverty in Zambia

Theme: #2
Competences: #1, 2 & 5

Key Words/Phrases

1. Agriculture
2. Development Plan
3. Quebec Model
4. Rural Poverty
5. Shanty-towns

Review Question/s

1. "Any solution that is designed to solve the shanty-town problem in Zambia must take into consideration the tripartite existence of a city, the shanty-town and the village." Discuss.

2. Propose a model under which shanty-towns may be transformed from instruments of death to creators of economic prosperity.

Multiple Choice

#1	What is the psycho-social damage that poverty may have on the nation?	Answer
A	Soul damage	
B	Poverty reduction	A
C	Disillusionment	
D	Entrepreneural acumen	

#2	Who was the first leader of Northern Rhodesia Congress which later became Northern Rhodesia Africa National Congress (NRANC), and who is considered to be the first leader of a national political party in Northern Rhodesia (Zambia)?	Answer
A	Goldwin Lewanika	
B	Kenneth Kaunda	A
C	Levi Manda	
D	Paul Kalichini	

#3	What does R.A.I stand for?	Answer
A	Rural Action Investment	
B	Road Action International	C
C	Rural Action International	
D	Rural Aid International	

#4	At independence, Zambia won all these, except _____	Answer
A	Political independence	
B	Diplomatic manumission	D
C	Self-determination	
D	Economic emancipation	

#5	The Scramble for Africa reveals that Europe was not interested in empowering Africans for _____	Answer
A	Self-sufficiency	
B	Self-disillusionment	A
C	Poverty	
D	Cultural disintegration	

#6	Zambian women and children deserve all these, except _____	Answer
A	Decent living standards	
B	Improved hygiene	D
C	Long life	
D	Poverty and disillusionment	

#7	Which IMF Managing Director in 2010 was impressed with the measures that Zambia had put in place to manage the economic crisis?	Answer
A	Christine Lagarde	
B	Horst Köhler	C
C	Dominique Strauss-Kahn	
D	Rodrigo Rato	

#8	What percentage of Zambian population was estimated by the LCMS IV of 2004 to fall below the poverty datum line?	Answer
A	64	
B	68	B
C	50	
D	60	

#9	What is the estimated percentage of poor people in Africa who live in rural areas and depend on agriculture for food?	Answer
A	50	
B	90	C
C	70	
D	40	

#10	What is the method used by the Jesuit Center for Theological Reflection (JCTR) to measure shanty-town poverty in Zambia?	Answer
A	Basic Needs Basket	
B	Basic Needs Baseline	A
C	Basket Needs Basement	
D	Basic Needs Bucket	

#11	What is the name of the system which involves cutting tree branches and burning them to act as crop manure?	Answer
A	Imyunda	
B	Impwa	C
C	Chitemene	
D	Rural Gardens	

#12	Who wrote the following: "The Western image, fostered by TV coverage of famine victims and advertisements for charity organizations, of sadness and despair, may have been true in extreme instances, but my experience of every class and types of Africans was that, everywhere and always, they would laugh and see the humor of life"?	Answer
A	Rodah Lester	
B	Index Mundi	D
C	Field Luwe	
D	William Grant	

#13	What was the approximate rate of life expectancy in Zambia in 2016?	Answer
A	38.63	
B	50	D
C	32	
D	52.36 years	

#14	Loss of productive workforce leads to all of the following, except _____	Answer
A	Loss of tax revenue	
B	Deepening poverty levels	C
C	High deficits	
D	High dependency ratios	

#15	Despite political independence, Zambia has faced all of these economic challenges, except _____	Answer
A	The mixed blessing of copper	
B	The orientation of the transport sector	B
C	The negligence of the manufacturing sector	
D	The negligence of the agricultural sector	

#16	The British Colonial Office decided to grant Zambian independence after _____	Answer
A	Depleting Northern Rhodesia of economic resources	
B	Bloodless struggle	A
C	Only 70 years of colonial rule	
D	The signing of the Barotseland Agreement, 1964	

#17	Who was Zambia's first university graduate?	Answer
A	John Mwanakatwe	
B	Mainza Chona	A
C	Nalumino Mundia	
D	Ronald Penza	

#18	When did Kenneth Kaunda announce the Mulungushi Reforms to restructure the economy in Zambia?	Answer
A	April 1969	
B	May 1970	D
C	March 1968	
D	April 1968	

#19	The omnibus parastatal created to oversee the other parastatals in 1972 in Zambia was _____	Answer
A	MINDECO	
B	FINDECO	D
C	INDECO	
D	ZIMCO	

#20	On which date was the Lusaka Stock Exchange launched into operation?	Answer
A	February 21st, 1994	
B	January 31st, 1995	A
C	February 21st, 1995	
D	January 31st, 1994	

#21	The three "Ls" promulgated by the Catholic Pope, Francis, in the fight against shanty-towns' conditions stand for _____	Answer
A	Land; Labor; and Lodging	
B	Land; Labor; and Living Accommodation	A
C	Land; Lodging; and Loyalty	
D	Labor; Land; and Loafing	

#22	Quebec stands out as a jurisdiction which has enacted a comprehensive poverty legislation whose purpose is to eradicate poverty. The core of the *Act to Combat Poverty and Social Exclusion* hinges mainly on _____ law.	Answer
A	Constitution	
B	Immigration	C
C	Human rights	
D	Corporate	

#23	It is a challenge to know exactly how many shanty-towns exist in Zambia because _____	Answer
A	They are too numerous to count	
B	More and more keep coming up every year	
C	They have no official councilor in the local government	B
D	Less and less records are kept in them	

#24	In this book, the issue of shanty-towns is approached from the point of view of _____	Answer
A	Causes and Effects	
B	Problems, analysis and solutions	
C	History	B
D	International Cooperation	

#25	Demolition of shanty-towns _____	Answer
A	Should be allowed	
B	Should be halted	
C	Should only be contemplated if there is a resettlement or replacement plan	C
D	Should not be contemplated because it is very expensive	

#26	Both the 2007-Mwanawasa Administration and the 2005-Zimbabwean Government orders to demolish shanty-towns backfired because _____	Answer
A	They were executive decisions	
B	They lacked a resettlement policy	
C	They were overly ambitious	B
D	They were apolitical	

Chapter 5| Pre-Independence Zambia

Theme: #1
Competence: #1

Key Words

1. Barotseland Agreement
2. Concession
3. Scramble
4. *Terra Nullius*
5. Treaty

Review Question/s

1. "Colonialism was founded on a very strong critical race theoretical base." Discuss.

2. Explain the four (4) significant colonial events that shaped the outlook of Zambia of today.

3. The hut tax was levied on all able-bodied males of 18 years old. Review the motivation and resultant impact of this practice on Northern Rhosedia (Zambia).

4. Captured chronologically, trace the progression of African sociopolitical organization to independence in this order: 1912 – Mwenzo Mission; 1946 – Federation of Welfare Societies; 1948 – Northern Rhodesia Congress; 1948 – African Representiatves Council; 1949 – African Mineworkers Union; 1952 – Northern Rhodesia African National Congress; 1958 – Zambia African National Congress; 1959 – United National Independence Party. Identify the persons involved and the issues encountered by these organizations.

Multiple Choice

#1	History can be discerned through all of the following, except _____	Answer
A	Vision	
B	Anthropology	A
C	Archaeology	
D	Oral myths and legends	

#2	Who is the grandfather of all known Bantu kingdoms?	Answer
A	Mierda	
B	Kazembe	A
C	Chiti-Mukulu	
D	Litunga	

#3	The descendants of Zambia laid claim to land primarily through conquests or _____, also known as the "Right of Soil."	Answer
A	*Jus Soli*	
B	*Jus Sanguinis*	A
C	Association	
D	Concession	

#4	In which year did Zambia become a British Protectorate?	Answer
A	1924	
B	1911	A
C	1964	
D	1890	

#5	Which treaty was signed on June 26th, 1890?	Answer
A	Lochner	
B	Ware	A
C	Lewanika	
D	Barotseland	

#6	When was the Barotseland Agreement concluded?	Answer
A	May 18th, 1964	
B	April 16th, 1964	A
C	October 23rd, 1964	
D	October 24th, 1964	

#7	Since 1925, the United States of America and the United Kingdom have scrambled for Zambia's copper. What was the first American company to prospect for Zambia's copper?	Answer
A	Roan Select Trust	
B	Anglo-American Corp.	A
C	British South Africa Company	
D	Konkola Copper Mines	

#8	Colonialism _____ Africa to the West.	Answer
A	Sold	
B	Exposed	A
C	Promoted	
D	Improved	

#9	Zambia's tourist potential is captured in the phrase _____	Answer
A	Let's Explore	
B	The Real Africa	A
C	One-Zambia, One-Nation	
D	Free for All	

#10	The scientific name for Kabwe Man is _____	Answer
A	Homo Rhodesiansis	
B	Broken Hill	A
C	Zinjanthropus	
D	Homo Habilis	

#11	Which Bantu people are believed to have been the first to inhabit present-day Zambia?	Answer
A	Ila	
B	Bushmen	A
C	Tonga	
D	Bemba	

#12	The period between the 16th and 19th centuries is known as _____	Answer
A	Iron Age	
B	Stone Age	A
C	Internet Age	
D	Dark Age	

#13	What type of doctrine is *Terra Nullius*?	Answer
A	Colonial	
B	Modern	A
C	Antiquity	
D	Slavery	

#14	The three ingredients of economic growth are ___	Answer
A	Capital; labor; land	
B	Capital; productivity; land	A
C	Labor; productivity; technology	
D	Land, water and technology	

#15	In which year was the Federation of African Welfare Societies formed?	Answer
A	1946	
B	1941	A
C	1948	
D	1952	

#16	What was the original name of MMD before Frederick Chiluba suggested otherwise?	Answer
A	National Interim Committee	
B	Movement for Democracy and Development	A
C	Central Interim Committee	
D	National Internal Committee	

#17	How did Kenneth Kaunda control parliamentary elections in the Second Republic?	Answer
A	He required candidates to be vetted by the Central Committee	
B	He required candidates to be vetted by the National Executive Committee	A
C	He required candidates to be vetted by the Secretary General of UNIP	
D	He required candidates to be vetted by the National Assembly	

#18	In which sense is the Barotseland Agreement, 1964, one of Zambia's instruments of independence?	Answer
A	It was concluded in 1964	
B	It was witnessed by the British Monarchy	
C	Without it Zambia would not have gone to independence as a unitary state	C
D	It involved the demarcation of land	

#19	Who popularized Indirect Rule in Africa?	Answer
A	Lord Frederick Lugard	
B	Lord Hailey	
C	John Cecil Rhodes	A
D	Gerald Caplan	

#20	When was the official policy on Indirect Rule adopted by the British Colonial Administration?	Answer
A	1928	
B	1929	
C	1922	A
D	1924	

Chapter 6| Struggles for Independence

Theme: #1
Competence: #1

Key Words

1. Federation
2. Freedom Fighter
3. Freedom Statue
4. Northern Rhodesia
5. Reparations
6. Resistance

Review Question/s

1. The Federation of Rhodesia and Nyasaland (the "Federation") was the last significant event before independence that would impact the political direction of Zambia. Explain two key factors that led to its creation and three factors that forced its dissolution.

2. List and explain three (3) similarities between the colonial regime in Northern Rhodesia and Apartheid in South Africa.

Multiple Choice

#1	Two of the Zambian fathers who epitomize the concept of sacrifice in the struggle for freedom in their books are_____	Answer
A	Mwaanga; Chisembele	
B	Mwaanga; Grey Zulu	B
C	Kaunda; Yamba	
D	Kaunda; Kapwepwe	

#2	The short-stubbing spear introduced by Shaka, King of the Zulus, is called _____	Answer
A	*Impi*	
B	*Assegai*	B
C	Sjambok	
D	Boko	

#3	The three (3) territories that made up the Federation of Rhodesia and Nyasaland were _____	Answer
A	Zambia; Malawi; Zimbabwe	
B	Northern Rhodesia; Nyasaland; Southern Rhodesia	B
C	Zambia; Southern Rhodesia; Nyasaland	
D	Northern Rhodesia; Zimbabwe; Malawi	

#4	The first crop of Africans who brought structure to the struggle for independence in Northern Rhodesia was former students; and they were stationed at _____ missionary institute.	Answer
A	Mwenzo	
B	Livingstonia	B
C	Mabel Shaul	
D	Tuskegee	

#5	In which year was the first welfare association formed; what was it called; and which two teachers instigated it?	Answer
A	1912; Mwenzo; Dauti Yamba and Donald Siwale	
B	1912; Mwenzo; Levi Mumba and Donald Siwale	B
C	1914; Livingstonia; Dauti Yamba and Levi Mumba	
D	1914; Livingstonia; Levi Mumba and Donald Siwale	

#6	Two of the politically-minded church leaders who laid the foundation for political agitation in Northern Rhodesia were _____	Answer
A	Edward Boti Manda and Grey Zulu	
B	David Kaunda and Hezekiya Nkonjera Kanoso	B
C	Peter Sinkala and Harry Mwaanga Nkumbula	
D	Kenneth Kaunda and Simon Mwansa Kapwepwe	

#7	In which year did Donald Siwale, Jonathan Mukwasa Simfukwe and Andrew Sichula transform the old Mwenzo Association into the Northern Rhodesia Native Association (NRNA)?	Answer
A	1914	
B	1923	B
C	1912	
D	1946	

#8	Which chartered company administered Northern Rhodesia on behalf of the British Government until 1924?	Answer
A	De Beers	
B	BSAC	B
C	Roan Antelope Trust	
D	Anglo-American Corp	

#9	Which person was tasked with the responsibility of inquiring into the disturbances in Northern Rhodesia before the British Government took over the administration of the chartered company in 1924?	Answer
A	Welesnky	
B	Judge McDonnell	B
C	Sir Evelyn Hone	
D	Malcolm MacDonald	

#10	In which year was Zambia African National Congress (ZANC) formed?	Answer
A	1959	
B	1958	B
C	1956	
D	1960	

#11	Zambia's first First Lady, Betty Mutinkhe Kaunda, died on _____	Answer
A	September 7th, 2012	
B	September 18th, 2012	B
C	September 18th, 2012	
D	November 18th, 2012	

#12	Which of the following was "one of the only four to vote against" the Federation of Rhodesia and Nyasaland in 1953?	Answer
A	Kenneth Kaunda	
B	Dauti Yamba	B
C	Donald Siwale	
D	Godfrey Miyanda	

#13	Which rival organization contrasted the British Colonial Office in both ideology and political interest during the colonial era before 1947?	Answer
A	Commonwealth Relations Office	
B	Dominion Office	B
C	Privy Council	
D	Dominion Affairs	

#14	Who was Britain's Secretary of State for Dominion Affairs during the colonial era in 1935, who was sympathetic to the interests of the Africans?	Answer
A	Godfrey Martin Huggins	
B	Lord Passfield	B
C	Sir Roy Welesnky	
D	Sir Gilbert Rennie	

#15	Godfrey Martin Huggins was the Prime Minister of Southern Rhodesia for _____ years.	Answer
A	3	
B	23	B
C	13	
D	5	

#16	Before the Federation of Rhodesia and Nyasaland, Southern Rhodesia was a self-governed state while Northern Rhodesia and Nyasaland were _____	Answer
A	Dominions of Britain	
B	British Protectorates	B
C	Overseas Territories	
D	Semi-Autonomy Enclaves	

#17	Which Tory British Prime Minister made the famous "Wind of Change" speech in the British South African Parliament in 1960?	Answer
A	Sir Arthur Edward Trevor Benson	
B	Harold Macmillan	B
C	Margaret Thatcher	
D	Tony Blair	

#18	Which Northern Rhodesian was part of the Walter Moncton Commission and who dissented against the continuation of the Federation of Rhodesia and Nyasaland?	Answer
A	Wellington Chirwa	
B	Habanyama	B
C	Maize Chona	
D	Nalumino Mundia	

#19	In 1962, the Africans won the majority in the Federal Legislative Council and made three (3) demands in view of Northern Rhodesia's cessation from the Federation. The following were the demands they made, except _____	Answer
A	Self-government	
B	Presidential democracy	B
C	A new constitution	
D	A new National Assembly	

#20	Who composed the song, "Independence Cha-Cha" which inspired the Cha-Cha-Cha Civil Disobedience Movement?	Answer
A	Nephas Tembo	
B	Joseph Kabasale	B
C	Isaac Santonga	
D	Sylvester Chisembele	

#21	The colonial identity cards called *Fitupas* were shunned by the Africans as symbols of _____	Answer
A	Colonialism	
B	Enslavement	B
C	Poor judgment	
D	British influence	

#22	Who was the first president of UNIP?	Answer
A	Kenneth Kaunda	
B	Dixon Konkola	B
C	Paul Kalichini	
D	Mainza Chona	

#23	On which date was the name "Zambia" coined in Lusaka's Chilenje Township?	Answer
A	October 24th, 1960	
B	October 24th, 1958	B
C	August 1st, 1953	
D	December 31st, 1963	

#24	Before independence, Zambia's Independence Avenue was known as _____	Answer
A	Queen Victoria Road	
B	King George Avenue	B
C	Prince Charles Blvd.	
D	Queen Elizabeth Way	

#25	The Freedom Statue picture portrait unveiled on October 23rd, 1974 is a true image of _____	Answer
A	Donald Siwale	
B	Mpundu "Zanco" Mutembo	B
C	Kapasa Makasa	
D	Dedan Kimathi	

Chapter 7| Independence Theories

Theme: #1
Competence: #3

Key Words/ Phrases

1. Democracy
2. Classical Liberals
3. Reform Liberals
4. Conservatives

Review Question/s

1. Illustrate by reference to the Lenshina Uprising the notion that self-motivated leaders who shaped public opinion on the need for political independence hailed from African independent churches.

2. Discuss the following view: "A people can only learn the art of governing, in part, by exercising it, and that it is

preferable to make one's own mistakes than to be governed by others, even if the mistakes are thereby greater."

Multiple Choice

#1	Liberals who lean towards the left-center are referred to as _____	Answer
A	Reform liberals	
B	Conservatives	A
C	Classical liberals	
D	Libertarians	

#2	The following three are among the six characteristics of conservatism identified by Russel Kirk, except_____	Answer
A	A strong belief in order	
B	Disbelief in order	B
C	A conviction that civilized society requires classes	
D	Distrust in economic abstraction	

#3	World War II exposed the Africans to _____	Answer
A	Europe	
B	Technology	C
C	Information	
D	Their roots	

#4	The critical year in which Britain began to no longer become aversed to granting the Africans political independence was _____	Answer
A	1889	
B	1924	D
C	1962	
D	1955	

#5	Which classical philosopher argued that human beings are by nature free?	Answer
A	Plato	
B	Aristotle	A
C	St. Augustine	
D	Aquinas	

#6	It is strongly construed that Zambia has met three critical factors that define democratic progress. Which of the following is not one of them?	Answer
A	A political culture	
B	Blameless leadership	B
C	A strong civil society	
D	A liberalized economy	

#7	Who made the assertion that, "A people can only learn the art of governing by exercising it, and that it is preferable to make one's own mistakes than to be governed by others, even if the mistakes are thereby greater"?	Answer
A	Plato	
B	Aristotle	C
C	John Stewart Mills	
D	John Locke	

#8	What, to Nietzsche, is the "the highest form of individual freedom, of sovereignty"?	Answer
A	A vote	
B	Political power	D
C	Veto power	
D	The will to power	

#9	The order of progression in the attainment of true freedom is _____	Answer
A	Freedom, Justice, Charity	
B	Freedom, Justice, Order	A
C	Charity, Justice, Freedom	
D	Charity, Freedom, Order	

#10	The best evidence that Africans were extremely competent and dependable in the administration of the colonial enterprise is from a _____	Answer
A	Song	
B	Poem	B
C	Dance	
D	Narrative	

#11	Imperial Britain had devised a course in *Africanization* in the 1950s _____	Answer
A	In preparation for the hand-over of power to the African government	
B	In preparation for the hand-over of power to the British government	A
C	In preparation for the training of new African leaders in political strategizing	
D	In preparation for World War III	

#12	Why was Colonial Britain suspicious of democracy in Africa?	Answer
A	It feared that Africa would dissolve into chaos	
B	It feared that Africa would be self-reliant	A
C	It had no confidence in the new African leadership	
D	It was ambivalent to the wishes of the settlers	

#13	The Mwenzo Association clearly stated in its 1923 constitution that independence was _____	Answer
A	Not one of its objectives	
B	Its major objective	A
C	One of its objectives	
D	Forseeable in a forseeable future	

#14	After World War II, the British Empire was _____	Answer
A	Externally weakened in power	
B	Internally weakened in power	B
C	Peripherially weakened in power	
D	Strategically weakened in power	

#15	Who postulated, thus, "A people under foreign domination are not free even if they may have their basic needs met by a foreign regime"?	Answer
A	Aristotle	
B	Plato	B
C	John Mills	
D	Adam Smith	

Chapter 8| The Second Republic

Theme: #1
Competences: #3 & 4

Key Words/ Phrases

1. Multiparty Democracy
2. One-Party State
3. One Party Participatory Democracy
4. Tyranny of the Majority
5. Dictatorship
6. Humanism
7. *Ubuntu*
8. Party and Its Government (PIG)
9. Chona Commission
10. Development Plan

Review Question/s

1. A political-democratic situation in which a government is democratically supported by most of its subjects because it makes policies or takes actions that only benefit that majority, while neglecting the rights and/or welfare of the rest of its subjects is a concept known as *Tyranny of the Majority*. Review the concept of One-Party Participatory Democracy under UNIP and explain how it relates to this concept.

Multiple Choice

#1	Two key themes identified in this chapter are _____	Answer
A	Poverty; oppression	
B	Oppression; democracy	B
C	Democracy; dictatorship	
D	Multiparty democracy; One-Party democracy	

#2	Which two major developments facilitated the creation of a One-Party State in Zambia?	Answer
A	Results of the 1967 elections; The Chona Commission	
B	Results of the 1967 elections; Prospects of the 1970 elections	B
C	Prospects of the 1970 elections; The Chona Commission	
D	The Chona Commission; Humanism	

#3	Which MP from Gwembe North stood as an independent after ditching ANC in or around 1964?	Answer
A	Arthur Wina	
B	Hugh Mitcheley	B
C	Sir Roy Welensky	
D	Harry Mwaanga Nkumbula	

#4	Who coined the phrase "Absolute power corrupts absolutely"?	Answer
A	Judge Denning	
B	Baron Acton	B
C	Abraham Lincoln	
D	William Shakespeare	

#5	What was the name of the political party that Simon Kapwepwe formed in 1972?	Answer
A	ANP	
B	UPP	B
C	ZANC	
D	UPL	

#6	Which section of *the Constitution (Amendment) (No.5) Act* of 1969 made the State of Emergency permanent in Zambia?	Answer
A	Section 7	
B	Section 8	B
C	Section 2(1)	
D	Section 4(1)	

#7	Which type of democracy is closest to representing the people's will?	Answer
A	Direct	
B	Referendum	B
C	One-Party Participatory	
D	Tyranny of the Majority	

#8	Who was convinced that the creation of the One-Party State was necessary to quail disturbances in Zambia?	Answer
A	VJ Mwaanga	
B	Grey Zulu	B
C	Alex Kamalondo	
D	Julia Kankasa	

#9	Who was the Deputy Chairman of the Chona Commission?	Answer
A	Mainza Chona	
B	Humphrey Mulemba	B
C	Nalumino Mundia	
D	Harry Nkumbula	

#10	Which Speaker of the National Assembly refused to recognize ANC as an official opposition in 1968?	Answer
A	Wesley Pillsbury Nyirenda	
B	Robinson Mwaake Nabulyato	B
C	Fwanyanga Matale Mulikita	
D	Amusaa K. Mwanamwambwa	

#11	The First National Development Plan in Zambia took place between _____ and _____.	Answer
A	1974; 1977	
B	1970; 1973	B
C	1978; 1983	
D	2006; 2010	

#12	What do we call cash payment towards the cost of mealie meal that the UNIP government gave to the Zambians?	Answer
A	A tax	
B	A subsidy	B
C	A grant	
D	A surplus	

#13	Who wrote the book, *Zambia Shall Be Saved* in 2001?	Answer
A	Nevers Mumba	
B	Kirbey Lockhart	B
C	Joe Imakando	
D	Oral Roberts	

#14	Why did the MMD hold their meeting at Garden House Motel in Lusaka on July 20th, 1990 instead of Livingstone City?	Answer
A	To avoid being close to Kenneth Kaunda's UNIP headquarters	
B	Due to lack of funds	B
C	To accommodate 130 delegates	
D	Because the owner offered the venue for free	

#15	Kaunda's Humanism recognized the supremacy of ____	Answer
A	God	
B	Man	
C	Kaunda	B
D	UNIP Central Committee	

#16	When did President Levy Mwanawasa and President Frederick Chiluba die, respectively?	Answer
A	August 19th, 2008; December 31st, 2009	
B	August 19th, 2008; June 18th, 2011	
C	July 18th, 2009; July 18th, 2011	B
D	August 18th, 2008; June 19th, 2011	

#17	UNIP's Central Committee controled the details of governance. For how many years did this go on?	Answer
A	19	
B	27	
C	18	A
D	26	

#18	What entrenched the concept of the Party and Its Government (PIG) under UNIP?	Answer
A	Its decision could not be challenged	
B	The Party was also the Government	
C	The Government was also the Party	A
D	UNIP and the Government of Zambia (GRZ) meant one and the same thing	

#19	Which Zambian president is naively considered to have ushered in a Fourth Republic?	Answer
A	Rupiah Banda	
B	Edgar Lunga	C
C	Michael Sata	
D	Frederick Chiluba	

#20	What defines a rulership whereby the elected majority, who only represents one political view, make all the decisions for a diverse nation?	Answer
A	Dictatorship	
B	Tyranny of the Majority	B
C	The Majority of One	
D	Indirect Rule	

Chapter 9| Coup Attempts

Theme: #1
Competence: #3

Key Words/Phrases

1. Coups d'état
2. Masterminds
3. Rape of the State
4. "Second" President
5. Cha-Cha-Cha

Review Question/s

1. President Mwalimu Nyerere once declared, "There is a devil in Africa." Why was this statement made? Discuss measures that African governments should put in place to avoid rampant coup attempts.

Multiple Choice

#1	Which Congolese was to organize a band of soldiers who would overthrow Kenneth Kaunda under the Shamwana-Musakanya coup plot?	Answer
A	Laurent Kabila	
B	Deogratias Symba	B
C	Moïse Katumbi	
D	Ben Mwila	

#2	Which Bank of Zambia Governor, in 1980, issued a public statement condemning the One-Party State?	Answer
A	Edward Shamwana	
B	Pierce Annifield	C
C	Elias Chipimo	
D	Valentine Musakanya	

#3	Who wrote the book, *Zambia's Most Famous Dissidents*?	Answer
A	Miles Larmer	
B	Venon Mwaanga	D
C	Elias Chipimo Junior	
D	Patrick Wele	

#4	What instigated the Shamwana-Musakanya coup attempt?	Answer
A	Mealie meal price hikes	
B	Continuation of a One-Party State	B
C	Fear of Kaunda's autocratic rule	
D	Dissatisfaction with the Chona Constitutional Review Commission	

#5	The Luchembe Coup took place on _____	Answer
A	June 30th, 1990	
B	June 30th,1980	A
C	October 5th, 1988	
D	May 28th, 1996	

#6	The following are alleged masterminds of the Shamwana-Musakanya coup plot, except _____	Answer
A	Godwin Mumba	
B	Anderson Mporokoso	D
C	Godfrey Miyanda	
D	Christon Tembo	

#7	The following are alleged masterminds of the October 1988 coup plot, except _____	Answer
A	Ben Mwila	
B	Bizwayo Nkunika	C
C	Laurent Kanyembu	
D	Wamulume Maimbolwa	

#8	Article _____ of the 1996 *Zambian Constitution* required any presidential candidate to prove that their parent/s were Zambian by birth or descent.	Answer
A	34(3)(b)	
B	37(3)(b)	A
C	34(3)(d)	
D	37(3)(d)	

#9	The coup attempt by Steven Lungu, a.k.a. Captain Solo of the Supreme National Council, took place on ____	Answer
A	May 28th, 1997	
B	October 28th, 1997	B
C	May 28th, 1996	
D	October 28th, 1996	

#10	Which Zambian employed guerrilla tactics to fight the UNIP government under Kenneth Kaunda and waged such war from around 1975 to November 26th, 1982, the date on which he was shot dead?	Answer
A	Alexander Saimbwende	
B	Adamson Mushala	B
C	Wilfred Wonani	
D	Donald Sadoki	

58

Chapter 10| Presidential Politics

Themes: #1, 2, 3, 4 & 5
Competences: #1, 2, 3, 4, 5 & 6

Key Words/Phrases

1. *Appropriation Act*
2. Cabinet
3. Chief Executive Officer (CEO)
4. Civil Control
5. Commander-in-Chief
6. Defence Council
7. Enabling Environment
8. Executive
9. For the President's Eyes Only
10. Judiciary
11. *Kapitao* Syndrome
12. Leader Principle

13. Legislature

14. Military Command

15. National Assembly

16. Office of the President (O.P)

17. Parliament

18. Separation of Powers

Review Question/s

1. "Military leaders are wired to dictate authority and command loyalty." This statement was made in the spirit of promoting democracy. Justify why in nations where the presidency is dominated by former military commanders the likelihood for undemocratic tendencies loom large.

2. For no fault of him, first Republican President, Kenneth Kaunda, was endeared with phrases such as "One Zambia, One Nation; One Nation, One Leader; that Leader, Dr. Kaunda *Wamuyayaya* (Forever), *Umutende* (Peace) *Na Ubuyantanshi* (and Development)." Other slogans were even more explicit, like: "In Heaven, God; On Earth, Kaunda!" In light of these phrases, what should be the attitude of Zambians towards the person who holds the Office of President?

3. List and explain the ten qualities women bring to law, politics and development.

Multiple Choice

#1	In Zambia, the president's office is also known as _____	Answer
A	O.P	
B	O.O.P	A
C	P.O	
D	P.O.O	

#2	The powers that the *Zambian Constitution* has assigned to the president may be characterized as _____	Answer
A	Excessive	
B	Complex	A
C	Deficient	
D	Arrogant	

#3	The division of powers among the Legislature, the Executive and the Judiciary is called _____	Answer
A	Separation of Powers	
B	Division of Powers	A
C	Branches of Government	
D	Levels of Government	

#4	Between 1964 and 1972, Zambia embraced a _____ system of government.	Answer
A	Multiparty	
B	One-Party	A
C	Socialist	
D	Customary	

#5	What is the Zambian Parliament?	Answer
A	National Assembly and the President	
B	150 MPs and the President	A
C	158 MPs and the Vice-president	
D	158 PMs and the President	

#6	The Zambian Parliament consists of _____ persons.	Answer
A	160	
B	158	A
C	150	
D	159	

#7	The highest power of the Zambian president is to _____	Answer
A	Uphold the Rule of Law	
B	Be Commander-in-Chief	A
C	Appoint the Cabinet	
D	Enforce Powers of Attrition	

#8	Which Zambian president was inaugurated on September 13th, 2016 after the Constitutional Court dismissed an opposition petition to nullify the elections held on August 11th, 2016?	Answer
A	Edgar Lungu	
B	Michael Sata	A
C	Guy Scot	
D	Rupiah Banda	

#9	The following is the summary of the Zambian presidential powers accorded to him/her by the constitution, except _____	Answer
A	Powers of attrition	
B	Constitutional fiat	D
C	Prerogative powers	
D	Powers of succession	

#10	To execute dates in relation to first sittings of Parliament, notice must be published in the _____	Answer
A	Hansard	
B	Gazette	B
C	Media	
D	Parliamentary Register	

#11	Where does the president derive the power to withdraw the money from the Consolidated Fund to meet expenditure when necessary?	Answer
A	The Constitution	
B	*The Appropriation Act*	B
C	Parliamentary Ratification	
D	*Consolidated Fund Act*	

#12	The Zambian Defence Force is composed of _____	Answer
A	Army and Air Force	
B	Army and Regular Force of the Army	A
C	Air Force and Air Force Reserve	
D	Auxiliary Air Force and Territorial Army Reserve	

#13	The Defence Council, which advises the president in matters of military policy, discipline and administration, is created by _____	Answer
A	The Defence Force	
B	The President	A
C	The National Assembly	
D	Joint Defence Chiefs	

#14	Four principles have necessitated Zambia's cordial relationship between the military and the civilian authorities, except _____	Answer
A	Having a civilian president as CEO	
B	The design of the defence forces	D
C	Apolitical nature of the military	
D	The Christian nature of Zambian presidency	

#15	Who is the chairperson of the Defence Council?	Answer
A	The Vice-president	
B	The Army Commander	C
C	The President	
D	Minister of Defence	

#16	In which year, and which government, subjected, for the first time in Zambian history, Estimate of Expenditure (Ministry of Defence) to Parliament?	Answer
A	1993; MMD	
B	2013; PF	A
C	2003; MMD	
D	1989; UNIP	

#17	Three of the following highlight the evidence that women can be better presidents than men; which one does not?	Answer
A	They are a weaker sex	
B	They are better performers	A
C	They grow and advance the economy	
D	They are more socially responsible	

#18	"The better informed the president is, the better decisions he or she will be able to make and the more secure and safe his or her state will eventually remain." This statement informs the notion of _____	Answer
A	Intelligence	
B	Order	A
C	Democracy	
D	Military-Civilian Synergy	

#19	Perceiving the president as a human being above reproach entails _____	Answer
A	*Kapitao* Mentality	
B	Leader Principle	B
C	Autocratic Rule	
D	Presidential Infallibility	

#20	Neo-Patrimonialism (client-patron relationship) is strongly imbued in _____	Answer
A	*Kapitao* Syndrome	
B	Leader Principle	A
C	Autocratic Rule	
D	Presidential Infallibility	

#21	The tendency to discriminate and ostracize women, historically, has resulted in all of the following, except _____	Answer
A	Not considered persons	
B	Had their feet bound	D
C	Were denied the right to vote	
D	Were never allowed to hunt	

#22	Which one of the following is NOT a view of hero-worship?	Answer
A	It defeats democracy	
B	It damns political pluralism and tolerance	D
C	It is pegged on the Leader Principle	
D	It did not exist in the Third Republic	

#23	Sikota Wina's comments that the name of the president should not be taken in vain and Simon Kapwepwe's assertion that President Kaunda was a man Zambia would never find again, illustrate _____	Answer
A	Leader Principle	
B	*Kapitao* Syndrome	A
C	Blind Loyalty	
D	Excessive Caderism	

#24	The president appoints, and is in charge, of all these commissions, except _____	Answer
A	Emoluments Commission	
B	National Lands Commission	A
C	The Medical Board	
D	State Audit Commission	

#25	Who appoints the Parliamentary Ombudsman in Zambia?	Answer
A	The president	
B	Parliamentary Service Commission	B
C	Police and Prison Services Commission	
D	Defence Council of Zambia	

Chapter 11| The Rule of Law

Key Words/Phrases

1. Amendments

2. Commoners

3. Constituent Assembly

4. Constitutional Review Commissions

5. Constitutionalism

6. Democrat

7. *Fiat*

8. Magna Carta

9. Rule of Law

10. Rule of Men

11. Separation of Powers

12. White Paper

Review Question/s

1. Review the statement: "The fact that the *Zambian Constitution* has been reviewed five times within a short space of fifty years shows that the nation is yet to enact a constitution that will stand the test of time."

2. "The Rule of Law should be above men." Discuss.

Multiple Choice

#1	The Magna Carta was a _____ document.	Answer
A	Federal	
B	Feudal	B
C	Imperial	
D	Colonial	

#2	The guarantee that, "No person shall be deprived of life, liberty and property, without due process," was derived from the _____	Answer
A	US Constitution, 5th Amendment	
B	Magna Carta	B
C	British Written Constitution	
D	Abraham Lincoln	

#3	Which of the following is not one of the principles established in the Magna Carta?	Answer
A	No-one is above the law	
B	The Monarch is supreme	B
C	Women have rights	
D	All humans have universal rights and freedoms	

#4	As established in this chapter, the Rule of Law must move in tandem with ____	Answer
A	The fight against the opposition	
B	The fight against crime	B
C	Parliament	
D	Capitalism	

#5	Each of the following is one of the ways the Rule of Law brings balance to society, except ____	Answer
A	Limiting the extent to which power can be used	
B	Giving the social weak the same rights as the strong enjoys	D
C	Official duty being done according to law	
D	Instilling the ideals of good government	

#6	To work, the law must ____	Answer
A	Be absolute and predominant	
B	Be used arbitrarily	A
C	Be a prerogative of the governors	
D	Award wide discretionary authority to government	

#7	What is defined as the performance of legislative functions by an organ that is independent of the executive and/ or party organ?	Answer
A	State power	
B	Legal power	B
C	Democracy	
D	The Rule of Law	

#8	When was the first Order-In-Council proclaimed in what came to be called Zambia?	Answer
A	1964	
B	1911	B
C	1916	
D	1967	

#9	The facets of Judicial Independence are the following, except _____	Answer
A	Absence of improper influence against judges	
B	Ratification of the Chief Justice	B
C	Impartiality of judges in decision-making	
D	Freedom of judges to do justice in their communities	

#10	Who was the first Chief Justice of Zambia?	Answer
A	Kenneth Kaunda	
B	James Skinner	
C	Sir Evelyn Hone	B
D	Earnest Sakala	

#11	What does the case of *Silva and Freitus v. The People,* illustrate?	Answer
A	Judicial power	
B	People power	
C	African power	B
D	State power	

#12	The *Inquiries Act* empowers government through ___	Answer
A	The Constitution	
B	A White Paper	
C	A Pink Paper	B
D	The Review Commissions	

#13	Zambia's return to multiparty politics was authorized by _____	Answer
A	Kenneth Kaunda	
B	*Constitution Act,* 1991	
C	*Constitution Act,* 1990	B
D	Westminster Model Constitution	

#14	What was the 2003 Mungo'mba Constitutional Review Commission also known as?	Answer
A	Pledged Constitutional Review	
B	Dragged Constitutional Review	B
C	Statutory Instrument Number 40 of 2003	
D	NCC Constitutional Review	

#15	What defines a good law?	Answer
A	By what it ought to be	
B	By what it does	B
C	By what it is	
D	By how many times it has been amended	

#16	The article famously titled "A Captive Chief Justice" pits a frucas between the judicial branch of government and the legal regulator, in which the Law Association of Zambia refused to endorse the Chief Justice's appointed judge by the name of ____	Answer
A	Mwamba Chanda	
B	Edward Luputa	A
C	James Chinyama	
D	Chilombo Maka	

#17	Is there such a thing as judicial independence?	Answer
A	Yes, because judges must be independent	
B	Yes, because courts must be independent	
C	Yes, because independence means judges and courts are free to do whatever they want	D
D	Yes, as far as judges' and courts' independence is tempered with a sense of responsibility and accountability	

#18	What does the standard of good behavior entail for judges?	Answer
A	That there is a steady administration of laws	
B	That there is an upright administration of laws	D
C	That there is an impartial administration of laws	
D	All of the above	

#19	"Rule of laws, not of men" implies each of the following, except _____	Answer
A	The governed should not be subjected to the discretion of the governors	
B	Both the governors and the governed should obey the same laws	D
C	Laws should be known, predictable and impartial	
D	Laws must be well-known to the governors only	

#20	What controversial provision of the *Zambian Constitution*, 1996 proscribed against candidates whose both parents were not Zambians by birth?	Answer
A	Section 129	
B	Section 34	C
C	Section 34(3)	
D	Section 129(3)	

Chapter 12| The Case of Human Rights

Theme: #5
Competence: #6

Key Words/Phrases

1. African Union
2. Human Rights
3. International Conventions
4. International Law

Review Question/s

1. Zambia is a signatory to most of the conventions that foster peace and human rights in Africa. What should be Zambia's role in ensuring that forced regime changes are terminated in Africa?

2. In the wake of recent developments in America where three diplomats were killed in Benghazi and the US demand for justice, how can modern students of African

peace designate the killing of Muammar Gaddafi? Provide a theoretical framework under which future proposed Western-backed regime changes must be managed in light of Africa.

Multiple Choice

#1	In which year was the African Charter and People's Rights adopted?	Answer
A	1981	
B	1963	
C	1961	A
D	2010	

#2	The following international instruments all safeguard against human rights abuses in Africa, except ___	Answer
A	The Security Council Resolution 1973	
B	Convention on the Prevention and Punishment of the Crime of Genocide	
C	International Convention on the Suppression and Punishment of the Crime of Apartheid	A
D	Convention Against Torture and Other Cruel, Inhuman or Degrading Treatment or Punishment	

#3	The AU's designation as having a history of failure saw its ascendance in _____	Answer
A	The Libyan war, 2011-2012	
B	The emergency of ISIS	
C	March of a Million, 2011	A
D	African propaganda for regime change	

#4	To change the AU from Organization of African Unity (OAU) several summits were held. Which summit drew the roadmap for the implementation of the AU?	Answer
A	Lusaka Summit 2001	
B	Durban Summit 2002	A
C	Sirte Summit 1999	
D	Lome Summit 2002	

#5	Which one of the following is NOT one of the components of the African Union mandate?	Answer
A	To eccelerate the process of integration in Africa	
B	To enable Africa to play a rightful role in the global economy	
C	To address multifaceted social, economic and political problems faced by Africa	D
D	To compound the negative image of Africa enabled by globalization	

Chapter 13| Naked before Government

Key Words/Phrases

1. Circumstantial Evidence
2. Communism
3. Mockery of Justice
4. Prisoner of Conscience
5. State of Emergency
6. The Other Society
7. Thoughts are Free

Review Question/s

1. Define a common thread that ties the following literary works, *The Other Society* by Vernon Mwaanga;

Thoughts are Free by Munyonzwe Hamalengwa; and *A Mockery of Justice* by Richard Sakala.

2. In **not** more than 1,500 words, compare and contrast the political legacy of the first five presidents of Zambia (Kenneth Kaunda; Frederick Chiluba; Levy Mwanawasa; Rupiah Banda; and Michael Sata) in that order.

Multiple Choice

#1	Why do centrist democrats and fiscal conservatives argue against a large government?	Answer
A	Because it is too complicated	
B	Because it is more efficient	C
C	Because it can become too powerful	
D	Because it tends to be one-person dominated	

#2	Chisala suggests that any of the following could have happened to anyone who was suspected of being disloyal to the UNIP Government, except _____	Answer
A	Detained	
B	Tortured	C
C	Reshuffled	
D	Blacklisted	

#3	Who was the first president of the 1972 Democratic People's Party?	Answer
A	Simon Kapwepwe	
B	Boniface Kawimbe	C
C	Fostino Lombe	
D	Davies Mwaba	

#4	When did Simon Kapwepwe die?	Answer
A	January 26th, 1981	
B	January 16th, 1980	C
C	January 26th, 1980	
D	January 17th, 1980	

#5	Who wrote the book entitled, *Thoughts are Free?*	Answer
A	Vernon Mwaanga	
B	Harry Nkumbula	C
C	Munyonzwe Hamalengwa	
D	Richard Sakala	

#6	U.N.I.T.A stands for _____	Answer
A	United for the National and Total Independence of Angola	
B	Unity and National Independence of Total Angola	C
C	National Union for the Total Independence of Angola	
D	National Union for the Independence of Total Angola	

#7	Under which statute was Nelson Mandela imprisoned?	Answer
A	*Preservation of Public Security Act*	
B	*Public Order Act*	C
C	*Suppression of Communism Act*	
D	Emergency Powers Ordinance	

#8	Colonial Britain established three sets of emergency powers for the territory that became known as Zambia. These were _____	Answer
A	Emergency Powers Order-in-Council 1940-61; Emergency Powers Ordinance, 1948; and Preservation of Public Security Ordinance, 1960	
B	Emergency Powers Order-in-Council 1939-61; Emergency Powers Ordinance, 1947; and Preservation of Public Security Ordinance, 1960	C
C	Emergency Powers Order-in-Council 1939-61; Emergency Powers Ordinance, 1948; and Preservation of Public Security Ordinance, 1960	
D	Emergency Powers Order-in-Council 1939-61; Emergency Powers Ordinance, 1948; and Preservation of Public Security Ordinance, 1961	

#9	Which three politicians were killed in similar circumstances in the Third Republic?	Answer
A	Michael Sata; Frederick Chiluba; and Levy Mwanawasa	
B	Michael Sata; Paul Tembo; and Baldwin Nkumbula	C
C	Wezi Kaunda; Paul Tembo; and Ronald Penza	
D	Ronald Penza; Levy Mwanawasa; and Baldwin Nkumbula	

#10	Which Catholic priest observed that the cruel way in which people were treated in Zambian prisons did not equal to the gravity of their offences?	Answer
A	Father "Red Card" Bwalya	
B	Bishop Elias Mutale	C
C	Father Given Mutinta	
D	Bishop John Mambo	

#11	All of these presidents dealt with or served under Kenneth Kaunda directly, except _____	Answer
A	Levy Mwanawasa	
B	Rupiah Banda	C
C	Edgar Lungu	
D	Michael Sata	

#12	All of these are some of the longest serving African presidents, except _____	Answer
A	Robert Mugabe	
B	Yoweri Museveni	C
C	Nelson Mandela	
D	Hosni Mubarak	

#13	Richard Sakala claims he was accused of stealing a second-hand motor vehicle and not of slander because ____	Answer
A	Slander is not bailable in Zambia	
B	Theft of motor vehicle is bailable in Zambia	
C	Theft of motor vehicle is not bailable in Zambia	C
D	Slander carries mandatory maximum sentence in Zambia	

#14	Mwanawasa's administration was christened _____	Answer
A	Cabbage administration	
B	Allergic to Corruption administration	C
C	New Deal administration	
D	Young Turks administration	

#15	According to Mwaipaya, what necessitates abuses of human dignity and rights?	Answer
A	Ignorance	
B	Fear	C
C	Ignorance and fear	
D	Nepotism and favoratism	

#16	All these happened around Simon Kapwepwe's death in January 1980. Which one did NOT happen?	Answer
A	He was tagged in a toga	
B	He was buried at Mwankole Hill	C
C	He was placed in a wooden casket	
D	No wreath was placed on his grave	

#17	At which prison did President Kaunda detain Munyonzwe Hamalengwa on February 9th, 1976?	Answer
A	Mumbwa	
B	Mukobeko	A
C	Lusaka Central	
D	Chilanga	

#18	The longest State of Emergency in Zambia was under President _____ and lasted from _____ to _____	Answer
A	Kaunda; 1964 – 1991	
B	Kaunda; 1953 – 1969	A
C	Chiluba; 1991 – 2001	
D	Chiluba; 1997 – 2000	

#19	What justifies the conclusion that there is a political murder?	Answer
A	That it is happening in a democratic country	
B	That there is a disproportionate number of high degree murders of politicians	B
C	That those who are being killed are former politicians	
D	That only non-ruling party politicians are being killed	

#20	Z.C.T.U stands for _____	Answer
A	Zambia Congress of Trade Unions	
B	Zambian Congress of Trade Unions	A
C	Zambia Company for Trade Unity	
D	Zambian Congress for Trade Unity	

Chapter 14| Criminal Reforms

Theme: #1

Competence: #6

Key Words/Phrases

1. Criminal Justice
2. Criminal Reforms
3. Prisons
4. Punishment

Review Question/s

1. "Prisons in Zambia are so overcrowded that inmates are sometimes forced to sleep seated or in shifts, and children behind bars are vulnerable to rape by adult prisoners.... Prisoners are starved, packed into cells unfit for human habitation, and face beatings at the hands of certain guards or fellow inmates. Children, pregnant women, pre-trial detainees, and convicted criminals are condemned to

brutal treatment and are at serious risk of drug-resistant TB and HIV infection." (a) Formulate means and ways of reforming the Zambian prisons; (b) In the light of the above statement, design a collaborative solution that involves Government, the civil society and the international community that is equipped to cure the present prison conditions in Zambia.

Multiple Choice

#1	How many prisons did Zambia have by 2011?	Answer
A	23	
B	67	D
C	5,500	
D	53	

#2	The reason why 1000 prisoners were released on parole in 2011 was in order to _____	Answer
A	Curb the rising inflation on prison budget	
B	Protect inmates from the spread of HIV-AIDS	D
C	Create new prisons	
D	Curb the problem of overcrowding	

#3	The observation that, "It is no longer the insane or social misfits that inhabit the cells. People in other countries have been known to acquire degrees and other forms of education while in cells – this means they access books and write and their minds are kept alive" stands for the proposition that _____	Answer
A	Prisons can be beautiful places	
B	Prisons can be centers of agitations	D
C	Prisons can be places for genius minds	
D	Prisons can be centers of knowledge and reformation	

#4	Who instigated the Unilateral Declaration of Independence (UDI) in Rhodesia?	Answer
A	Robert Mugabe	
B	John Cecil Rhodes	D
C	Joshua Nkomo	
D	Ian Douglas Smith	

#5	Who said these words: "True patriotism hates injustices in its own land more than anywhere else"?	Answer
A	Clarence Darrow	
B	Martin Luther King, Jr.	A
C	Harry Nkumbula	
D	Puta Chekwe	

Sample Lesson PowerPoint Slide

1. Zambian Independence

- **Mibenge**
- A village in one of the 10 provinces of Zambia, Luapula Province
- Comprises several small villages
- **October 24th, 1983**
- Zambia's 19th independence anniversary
- Great celebrations
- *Bamwisa* (foreigners, colonialists)
- *Abasungu* – people who move around

1. Zambian Independence (Cont.)

- **October 23rd, 1964**
- Independence Stadium – along Lusaka-Kabwe Road
- Kenneth Kaunda – Prime Minister of Northern Rhodesia; first President of Zambia
- Her Royal Highness Princess Royal – representing the Queen of England
- Founding Fathers – Zambia's "A" Team
- **Struggles of the Zambians**
- Struggles for Independence
- Independence

List of Five Themes

#1

That democracy and development in Zambia cannot be adequately defined without taking into consideration Zambia's uniqueness and historical factors that impact upon its culture, society and future well-being;

#2

That a definite change of mind-set is essential if Zambia is to manipulate its people, natural and financial resources into productivity;

#3

That generational disparity exists in Zambian leadership formation that affects the choice of developmental models and for the most part, limits its investment, innovativeness and technological proficiency;

#4

That a combination of, or hybrid, ideological and pragmatic approach is necessary to unlocking Zambia's economic potential; and

#5

That a belligerent approach espoused by the International Financial Institutions, Cooperating Partners and the donor governments pre-empts Zambia's most coveted inventiveness, sophistication and free experimentation.

List of Six Competences

#1

To demonstrate an understanding of the history of Zambia;

#2

To demonstrate an understanding that the growth and stability of the Zambian economy depends on the critical scrutiny of past and present developmental models and the appreciation of the national-specific nuances that have a direct impact upon the strategies and mechanism that must aim at the eradication of poverty and social disillusionment;

#3

To demonstrate an understanding and appreciation of the necessity of respect for, and audacious pursuance of, democratic tenets and their impact on political development;

#4

To demonstrate the necessity for adherence to, and the appreciation for, liberty in the framework of human rights, freedom and inter-tribal amity as basis for national development, social integration and political and cultural hegemony;

#5

To understand and appreciate that the inculcation of sound moral and ethical good through education, religion and conscience are key to the unlocking of potential, leading to enlightenment, spiritual ascendancy and human actualization;

#6

To demonstrate the understanding that law and the rule of law are cardinal in the ordering and stabilizing of society and the general good.

Notes